THE BATTLE FOR ARNHEM

The Prelude to Market Gard

After the success of the invasion of Normandy on 6 June 1944, in which the 82nd and 101st US Airborne and the 6th British Airborne Divisions played a vital part, a long battle led to the liberation of Paris on 25 August.

From 1 September the overall command of Allied operations was under General Dwight D. Eisenhower at Supreme Headquarters Allied Expeditionary Forces (SHAEF) with three Army Groups reporting to him: Field Marshal Montgomery's 21st, Lt-General Omar Bradley's 12th and Lt-General Jacob Devers's 6th. Lines of supply still depended on the ports of Normandy, and Montgomery and Bradley vied for priority in the allocation of vital resources. While Montgomery made his case for support in the pursuit of the crumbling German resistance in northern France and Belgium, Bradley quietly continued to back Patton's dramatic thrust eastwards. Generalfeldmarschall Walther Model struggled to organise the remains of German Army Group B but the British and Canadians swept forward. Lt-General Brian Horrock's XXX Corps took Brussels on 3 September and Antwerp the day after, but the lines of supply were being stretched even longer.

Although th… Channel ports, th… waterways of the Scheldt estuary, without wh… p was closed, was not sufficiently appreciated, and the advance halted. It was then, on 10 September, that Montgomery proposed a daring strike north to outflank the German Rhine defences by securing bridgeheads all the way from the Belgian border to the town of Arnhem on the Lower Rhine. With the 1st Allied Airborne Army under Lt-General Brereton in England awaiting deployment, it was an idea that found favour. Lt-General F.A.M. Browning and the associated commanders had only one week to plan and launch the 100km (60 miles) thrust by XXX Corps (code-named Operation Garden) from the Belgian border to link with the airborne troops (Operation Market) of the 101st US Airborne Division north of Eindhoven on the first day, 82nd US Airborne at Nijmegen on the second and the 1st British Airborne at Arnhem on the third.

Below: This Chain of Command diagram shows only those units on the battleground, omitting the RAF, USAAF, etc.

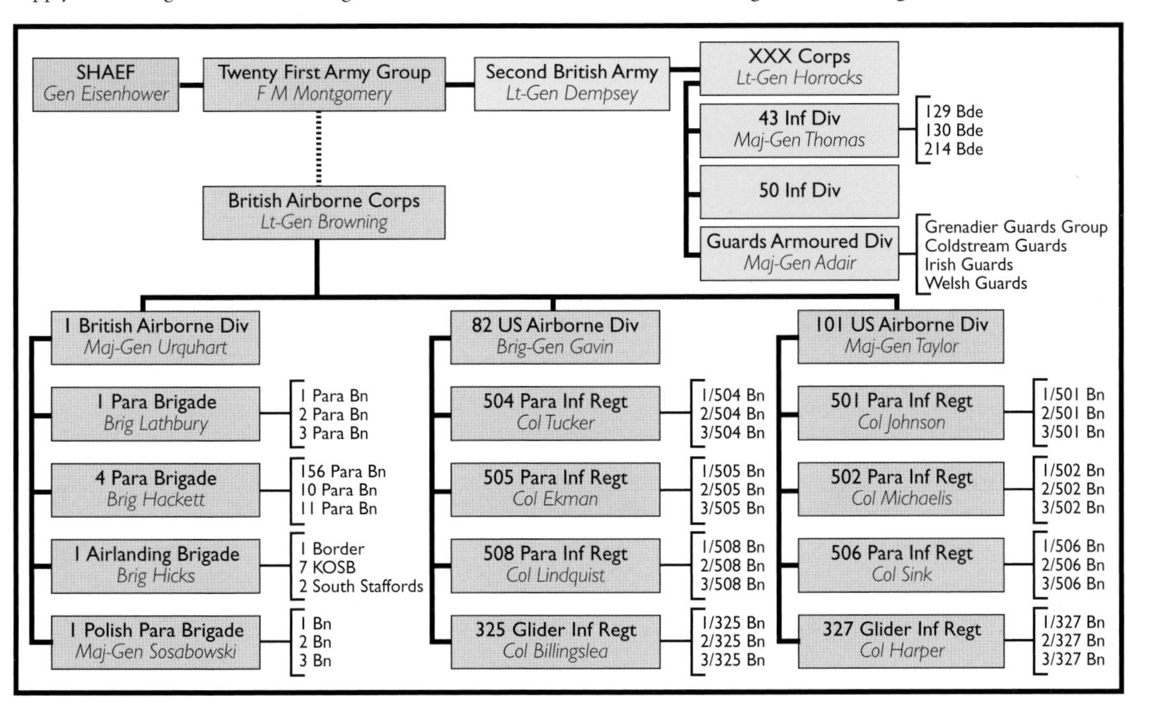

17 September 1944 – The 1st British Airborne Division

When Model received the news of the airborne landings, he rushed to the headquarters of Obergruppenführer Willi Bittrich's II SS Panzer Corps at Doetinchem, to the east of Arnhem. As the Allies knew, Bittrich was supervising the refitting of 9th and 10th SS Panzer Divisions, though the 9th had just been ordered to return to Germany. In the planning they had been unwisely dismissed as broken formations.

The 1st Airborne, under the command of Major-General R.E. Urquhart, consisted of 1st Parachute Brigade (Brigadier Lathbury), 4th Parachute Brigade (Brigadier Hackett), 1st Airlanding Brigade (Brigadier Hicks) and, for this operation, 1st Polish Independent Parachute Brigade (Major-General Sosabowski). The fear of flak – anti-aircraft fire – from Arnhem and Deelen led to the selection of landing zones (LZs) and drop zones (DZs) well to the west of the objective of the bridge at Arnhem (see map page 10/11), and the shortage of aircraft and crew meant that it would take three lifts over three days to move the entire division into the area.

At 12.40 p.m. the Pathfinders, the 21st Independent Parachute Company, dropped to mark LZ-S north-west of Wolfheze and LZ-Z and DZ-X south west of the village, which was still smoking from the bombing intended to hit anti-aircraft guns. Over 80 civilians were killed. Twenty minutes later the gliders began to arrive on the LZs and by 2 p.m. the parachutes were opening over the DZ. This first lift brought 1st Parachute Brigade, 1st Airborne Reconnaissance Squadron, Urquhart and his staff and most of 1st Airlanding Brigade. The latter were to secure the LZs and DZs for future landings, while the men of the 1st Border Regiment moved to cover the zones to the south, the 7th King's Own Scottish Borderers (KOSB) moved west and the 2nd South Staffordshire gathered to defend LZ-S. There had been remarkably small losses on the way as a result of the 1,395 bomber and 1,240 fighter sorties flown in advance of the lifts. Casualties on landing were also mercifully few, although two of the clumsy Hamilcar gliders, carrying heavy equipment, dug in and overturned while some of the lighter Horsas collided. The landings were virtually unopposed.

Below: A Horsa glider on tow. The 29-man glider was side-loading and could also carry jeeps and field guns. (IWM)

The speed with which the troops organised themselves was remarkable and 1st Para's three battalions each linked with their troop of four 6-pounder anti-tank guns to move off, but first Major Freddie Gough's Recce Squadron was ordered to make a dash for the bridge by way of a track just north of the railway line. They did not get far – a training battalion under Sturmbannführer Kraft had covered the railway and Wolfhezerweg, and stopped the Squadron east of Wolfheze. Meanwhile 3rd

Right: The modern Driel ferry approaching the pier below Westerbouwing. In the distance the Den Brink tower is on the left, the railway bridge on the right. (MME)

Background: Drop Zone X, south-west of Wolfheze, on 17 September, peppered with parachutes. (IWM)

Above: Civilians welcome 3 Section, A Troop, 1st Airborne Reconnaissance Squadron in Backerstraat, Oosterbeek, on 18 September. (Van Woerkom/AM)

Battalion were making their way along the Utrechtseweg where they shot up the staff car of General Friederich Kussin. As they approached the Bilderberg Hotel they ran into Battalion Kraft and a series of small actions pinned them down until nightfall when they made it as far as the Hartenstein Hotel. The Divisional and the Brigade commanders, unable to communicate by radio, had taken to rushing about in jeeps to find out what was going on, thus largely removing themselves from their commands.

1st Battalion were to secure the northern approach to Arnhem and started along Amsterdamseweg. They soon ran into elements of 9th Panzer but, as afternoon turned to evening, they heard, in a brief moment of radio clarity, that 2nd Battalion were at the bridge. Having suffered the loss of some 100 men, they headed south-east in an attempt to join them.

Lt-Colonel John Frost received orders to move off with his 2nd Battalion at 3 p.m. and made his way through Heelsum and Doorwerth to take the riverside road to Arnhem. They were delayed at Oosterbeek by the welcome they had from the Dutch. The railway bridge was blown up by the Germans just as C Company reached it. From the bridge the railway swings up and to the east into Arnhem on the heights of Den Brink, now crowned with a telecommunications tower. From that height the Germans directed machine-gun and armoured-car fire on A Company as they attempted to pass the rail embankment by the road tunnel. B Company engaged the enemy as, in the failing light, Frost's men pushed on into the town. The pontoon bridge, where the new road bridge now crosses the river, was partially dismantled, denying access to the southern bank. In the dark Frost kept moving, but was limited to seizing the northern approach ramp to the road bridge and the surrounding houses, where he was joined by Brigade HQ except for Lathbury and by Gough with two jeeps of the Recce Squadron. An attempt to cross the bridge was halted by fire from a tower.

At about 10 p.m. an anti-tank gun was in position to shell it and a flame-thrower was used as well, igniting ammunition nearby. The blaze lit up the area for hours and set fire to a German convoy trying to cross. Mission, in part, accomplished.

Left: German troops in Stationsweg, Oosterbeek, make haste to camouflage their vehicles before moving off to oppose the landings on 17 September. In spite of the surprise of the airborne attack, the Germans were remarkably resourceful in their reaction. (A.F. Kremer/AM)

Above: Brigadier-General Jim Gavin preparing for departure with his 82nd Airborne Division on 17 September. (USSC)

17 September – The US 82nd Airborne Division

Brigadier-General Jim Gavin's 82nd Airborne, the 'All American', were tasked with the seizure of the crossings of the Maas at Grave and the Waal at Nijmegen and of the canal between them (see map, back cover). The DZs and LZs allocated were even further from his objectives than those of the British at Arnhem, but once more fear of flak led the airmen to insist on these locations. South-east of Nijmegen the wooded hills along the German border rise steeply between the rivers and here 508th Parachute Infantry Regiment, a unit the size of a British brigade, landed east of a line from Groesbeek to Berg en Dal. To their south, between Groesbeek and Mook, 505th were dropped while 504th's DZ was between Heumen and Grave, with one company landing south of the Maas at Grave. Attacked from both sides, the bridge at Grave was soon in American hands as, by the end of the day, was the Maas-Waal Canal bridge at Heumen, where the link with 505th was made.

The tasks of 508th were many. Not only did they have to prepare to defend against an attack by German troops from the east along the northern flank of the Groesbeek Heights, but they also had to move west to help secure bridges over the canal. Further, Gavin had given vague orders to have a crack at the Nijmegen bridges should the chance arise. This last objective was denied them late that evening when they ran into elements of 9th Panzer which Bittrich, using the ordinary telephone lines, had ordered south from Arnhem before Frost closed the bridge. In spite of this shortfall the American achievement was highly successful.

17 September – The US 101st Airborne Division

The 'Screaming Eagles', the 101st Airborne under Major-General Maxwell Taylor, had to secure the southernmost section of the road up which Operation Garden would unroll, a road that became known as Hell's Highway. 502nd and 506th Parachute Infantry Regiments dropped and landed north of the Sonse Forest between Son and St Oedenrode while 501st were put down south west of Veghel. Son fell to 506th but as the Americans moved south towards the bridge on the Wilhelmina canal the Germans blew it up. It was midnight before a makeshift wooden structure had been built and, cautious about attempting to enter a city in the dark, 506th dug in north of Eindhoven, an objective scheduled to be taken within two hours of landing.

The bridge over the Wilhelmina canal to the west at Best was a target of 502nd Regiment, but they came under fire and also dug in for the night. Further north 502nd succeeded at the Dommel bridge at St Oedenrode and at Veghel 501st took both the canal and river bridges. The 101st were off to a good start.

Below: In England heavily laden parachute troops of the 82nd Airborne make ready to board a C-47, also known as the Dakota, of the 61st Troop Carrier Group to be flown to their drop zone near Nijmegen. (USSC)

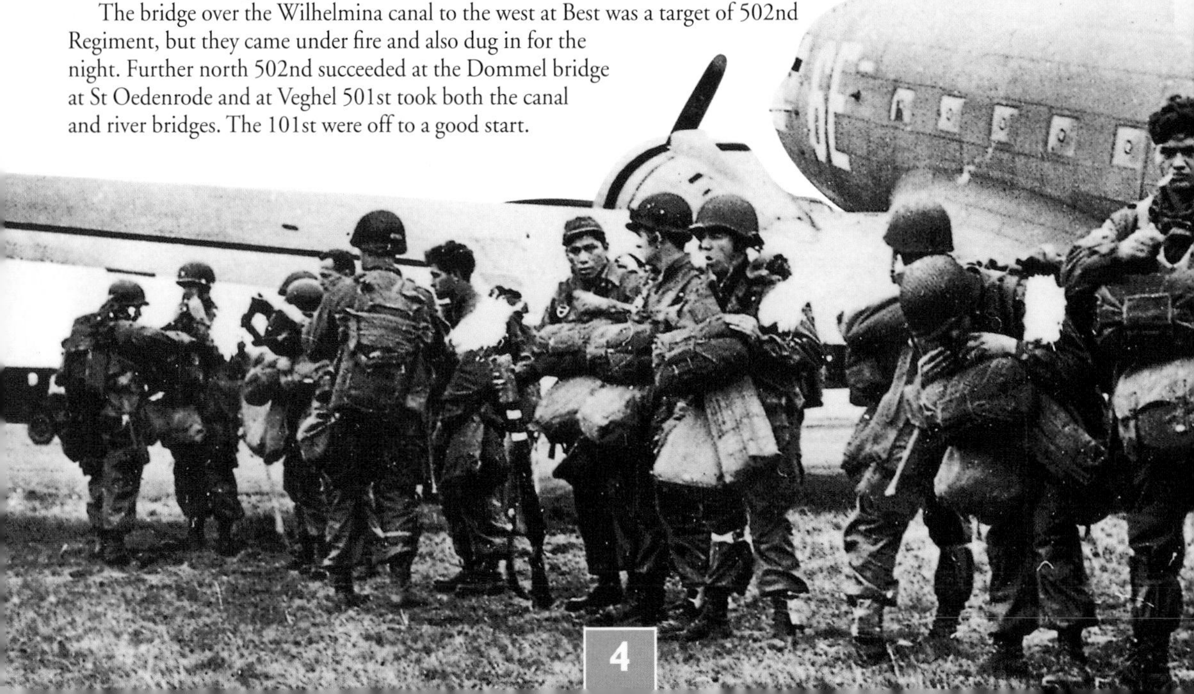

Right: The British were wary of the advice of the Dutch resistance as a result of the penetration by the Germans earlier in the war. The Americans gained much from their more open approach. Here, at Veghel on 17 September, a member of PAN, Partizanen Actie Nederland, assists men of the 101st Airborne. (USSC)

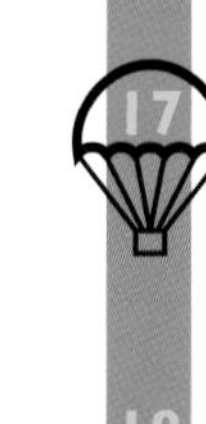

Left: The bridge at Grave, a vital link in the line of approach of XXX Corps, was taken by the 82nd Airborne on 17 September. Here it is guarded by men of the Dutch Prinses Irene Brigade. (AM)

Below: The Dome of Honour, Liberation Museum, Groesbeek adds to the museum's coverage of the Second World War in the Netherlands a complete record of Allied service men and women who gave their lives from D-Day to the end of the war. (MME)

17 September – XXX Corps

As Operation Garden started Lt-General Brian Horrocks was well aware of the challenge his XXX Corps faced. German resistance had hardened during the dash across Belgium and the first 15 minutes of the advance from the Meuse-Escaut canal confirmed this – nine tanks of the Guards Armoured Division were already in flames. Rockets from RAF Typhoons directed by radio and artillery fire smashed into German strong-points and the tanks rolled forward once more. The co-ordination was near perfect and by nightfall the Guards had liberated Valkenswaard. But this was 10km (6 miles) south of Eindhoven, their objective for the first day. Already the pace of XXX Corps was dropping below expectations.

Above: Deep skid-marks attest to the impact of gliders on Landing Zone S, clearly marked to assist the pilots. (IWM)

Left: The Arnhem road bridge, photographed on 18 September. The wreckage of the German convoy that attempted to cross from the south can be seen at the northern end of the bridge. At that time houses, used by the British, crowded close to the northern ramp. (IWM)

Right: A Jeep of the 2nd Battalion, South Staffords makes its way along Utrechtseweg on 18 September, towing a 6-pounder field gun. (Caspers/AM)

18 September – 1st British Airborne

There was a mixed force of some 740 British troops around the north end of the bridge at Arnhem to view the smoking remains of the German lorries on Monday morning, nearly half of them members of Frost's 2nd Battalion. They had occupied houses flanking the roadway which rose to the bridge, first across an earth embankment and then on pillars. They waited. Lorries containing German troops strayed into the area in front of Frost's HQ and were shot up, then at about 9.30 a.m. 9th SS Panzer's Reconnaissance Battalion, sent south towards Nijmegen the previous day, attempted to return over the bridge. A few armoured cars got through, but the rest of the force, including half-tracks full of troops, was destroyed, leaving the highway filled with burning equipment and slaughtered men. A tank attack on their eastern flank was repelled by the British with support from the 75-mm guns in Oosterbeek, and smaller actions continued during the rest of the day, a steady rain of sniper and mortar fire that would persist to the end.

The German reaction to the landings was swift and decisive. Two blocking lines were set up by Ludwig Spindler to cover the west of the town, one of them less than 1000m (1100yd) from the bridge itself.

Early in the morning the 3rd Battalion moved forward from the Hartenstein Hotel to try the riverside road. Enemy fire was intermittent. The mortars, Vickers machine-guns and three of their four guns got separated and so Lt-Colonel Fitch found himself without this vital support when they reached the Pavilion, a riverside building behind the modern Rijnhotel. Attempts to advance were prevented by fire from a self-propelled gun (SPG) and by artillery at the brickworks on the south bank. The impasse lasted until 4 p.m. when the decision was taken to move north. They filtered through the houses west of St Elisabeth's Hospital. Urquhart, Lathbury and Lieutenants Taylor and Cleminson became separated in the maze of little streets. Lathbury was wounded and pulled into a house. The others dodged down an alley and into Zwarteweg 14. The presence of a German SPG isolated them there for the next 12 hours.

The 1st Battalion also headed south that day, following the same line as the 3rd but running into much stronger resistance on passing under the railway bridge on the lower road. They fought their way through to end up just west of the hospital. With Urquhart missing, the divisional command passed to Brigadier Hicks. At about 10 a.m. he decided to send the South Staffords to support the effort to reinforce the bridge, and to take the 11th Battalion from 4th Parachute Brigade, once it arrived, to add to them. By 9 p.m. the South Staffords had joined 1st and 3rd Battalions.

The second airlift was to bring the remainder of the 1st Division out, except the Poles. It was delayed by fog in England and the landings took place late, soon after 3 p.m., at DZ-Y,

LZ-X and LZ-S. By now the Germans had rallied enough to offer some resistance, but 7th Battalion KOSB dealt with it. Brigadier Hackett was less than pleased to learn that 4th Parachute Brigade was to yield 11th Battalion at once, but they, too, followed the riverside route into Arnhem and were in touch with their comrades by midnight. Hackett was supposed to use his brigade to occupy ground north of Arnhem, but now had to deal with significant casualties. As night fell his 156th and 10th Battalions moved forward north of the railway but ran into fire near Dreijenseweg, the road running north from Oosterbeek station, and withdrew for the night. The KOSB just north of them at Johannahoeve had a similar experience. They did not know they had located the second German blocking line.

18 September – 82nd and 101st US Airborne

To the south progress was slow. Warned by the Dutch resistance, Gavin recalled 508th Regiment from Nijmegen to protect the LZs from German attack, just before the arrival of the second lift. Mook was taken by 505th but the Honinghutje bridge on the Maas–Waal canal was blown up just as men of 504th and 508th were taking it, so a detour through Heumen was going to be necessary later.

Eindhoven was entered by 101st's 506th Regiment by noon, but at Best 502nd ran into the German 59th Division and suffered fearfully. At 11 a.m. the Best bridge was blown, joining the Son bridge in ruins.

Right: The alley off Zwarteweg from which a path leads to the rear of number 14. (MME)

18 September – XXX Corps

The Irish Guards were on the move at 6 a.m., but without air support, the result of fog at the airfields in Belgium. Their advance was a long, hard grind. It was not until 5.30 p.m. that the tanks clanked through Eindhoven and out towards Son, where work to repair the bridge started that evening.

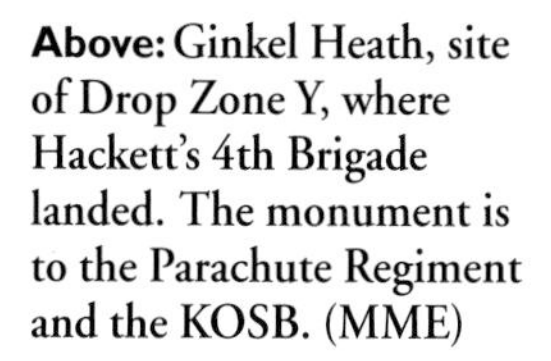

Above: Ginkel Heath, site of Drop Zone Y, where Hackett's 4th Brigade landed. The monument is to the Parachute Regiment and the KOSB. (MME)

Right: The rebuilt road bridge at Arnhem, named after Lt-Colonel John Frost. The structure on the right is the site of the tower attacked on 17 September. (MME)

Left: Defiant in defeat, the captured Lt J. Reynolds makes a rude gesture at the photographer. He commanded the 1st Platoon Mortar Group of the 2nd Battalion, South Staffords. The German soldier to the left is pushing a Flying Flea, a miniature motor-bike used by the British. (B)

19 September – 1st British Airborne

Tuesday brought no relief to the men at the Arnhem bridge. As the day wore on the German attacks built in ferocity, their SPGs and tanks adding their fire to the mortars and machine-guns.

A false report that the bridge had fallen prompted Hicks, at 1 a.m., to order 1st and 3rd Battalions and the South Staffords to withdraw but the error was corrected and it was planned that the 1st and 3rd would attack along the riverside road while the South Staffords would advance along the upper road past St Elisabeth's Hospital with the 11th Battalion coming up behind them. Meanwhile the Germans had reorganised their defence, a move that incidentally freed Urquhart from his hiding place. The 1st and 3rd moved off at 4 a.m. and managed to reach the eastern end of the open ground before being stopped by fire from three sides. By 6.30 they were dead, wounded or on the point of becoming prisoners. The South Staffords started at 4.30 a.m., and managed to reach the area of the municipal museum. When their PIAT (Projectile, Infantry, Anti-Tank) ammunition was gone the tanks moved in and their numbers were steadily reduced.

The 11th were ready to help, but Urquhart, seeing his men being dribbled away, ordered them to take the high ground beyond the railway to open the way for 4th Parachute Brigade. Elements of the South Staffords took Den Brink to support their flank, but the 11th never got the chance to move; German fire cut them to ribbons. The bridge could not be reinforced. The tanks rolled west and the remnants of the British, about 500 men, fell back to Oosterbeek.

At 1.30 p.m. Urquhart went to Hackett's HQ at Johannahoeve and, unaware of the adverse situation in Arnhem, it was decided that 4th Brigade would withdraw south of the railway embankment preparatory to moving into Arnhem. The move took place under increasing pressure from the Germans, and as it did so, at about 4 p.m., the delayed and depleted third glider lift started to land. The Polish soldiers found themselves in the middle of a battle, unable to tell who was who and sometimes themselves mistaken for Germans. The 10th Battalion had to move back to Wolfheze to cross the railway, though many found a route through a drainage tunnel just west of the modern motorway. The Brigade gathered south of the railway for the night, having been covered by rearguard actions by the KOSB and some men of the 10th under Capt. Queripel. He died in doing so and was awarded the Victoria Cross. The day's supply flights left only 31 tons in British hands of the 390 tons dropped. The Oosterbeek enclave was forming.

Below: German soldiers climb the railings of the Municipal Museum in Arnhem, which was occupied by elements of the South Staffords. (B)

19 September – 82nd and 101st Airborne with XXX Corps

The Household Cavalry crossed the new Bailey bridge at Son at dawn, but the threat to Hell's Highway from the west by the German 59th Division at Best had not been averted. Horrocks gave Taylor the 15th/19th Hussars to support a fresh attack by 506th Regiment and 327th Glider Infantry. They were successful, taking over 1,000 prisoners, and liberating the remnants of the 502nd, but not PFC Joe E. Mann. He had died protecting his comrades by throwing himself on a grenade lobbed into his trench. He was awarded the Congressional Medal of Honour. Taylor then had to deal with a late afternoon attack from the east by 107th Panzer Brigade. The third lift had reached him in spite of the heavy cloud and fog, making available artillery to throw the Panzers back, but the whole length of the road held by the 101st was continuously subjected to other, smaller attacks.

The Guards Division made it to Grave by mid-morning, but had to go by way of Heumen so that it was afternoon before they could join 82nd's 505th Regiment to attack the bridges at Nijmegen. The approaches through the town were fraught with hazard; the ancient fortification just south-west of the road bridge, the Valkhof, was heavily manned and the Germans had reinforced their defence with men ferried over the Pannerdens canal. The attack failed. Gavin then proposed the plan of a water-borne crossing, but the canvas boats were far in the rear so it could not be done that night. It would have to be done in daylight. The Waal bridges were still in German hands and on this day, Tuesday, XXX Corps should have been at Arnhem.

Right: St Elisabeth's Hospital was at the heart of the fighting on 19 September. A Red Cross flag flew from it and, throughout the battle, the Germans gave passage to Red Cross Jeeps and British walking wounded seeking aid. When the 1st Airborne fell back to Oosterbeek, medical officers and staff of 16 Parachute Field Ambulance continued treatment of the casualties with Dutch help. (MME)

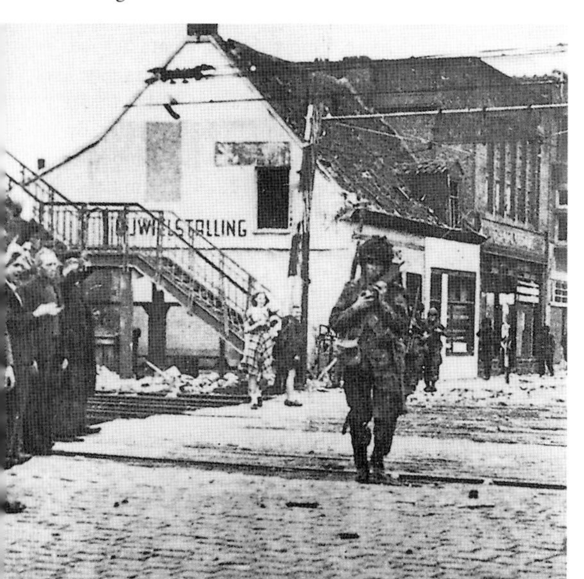

Above: Civilians wave a welcome to men of the 2nd Battalion, 506th Regiment, 101st Airborne as they move north. (USSC)

Right: The grave of Flight Lieutenant David Lord, VC, DFC, one of the men killed in the effort to resupply the 1st Airborne, in the CWGC Cemetery at Oosterbeek. He continued to fly his burning aircraft to complete his drop before the wings gave way. (MME)

Above: A plaque on the wall of a house on the north of Utrechtsestraat, east of the Municipal Museum. (MME)

The Battle at Arnhem and Oosterbeek

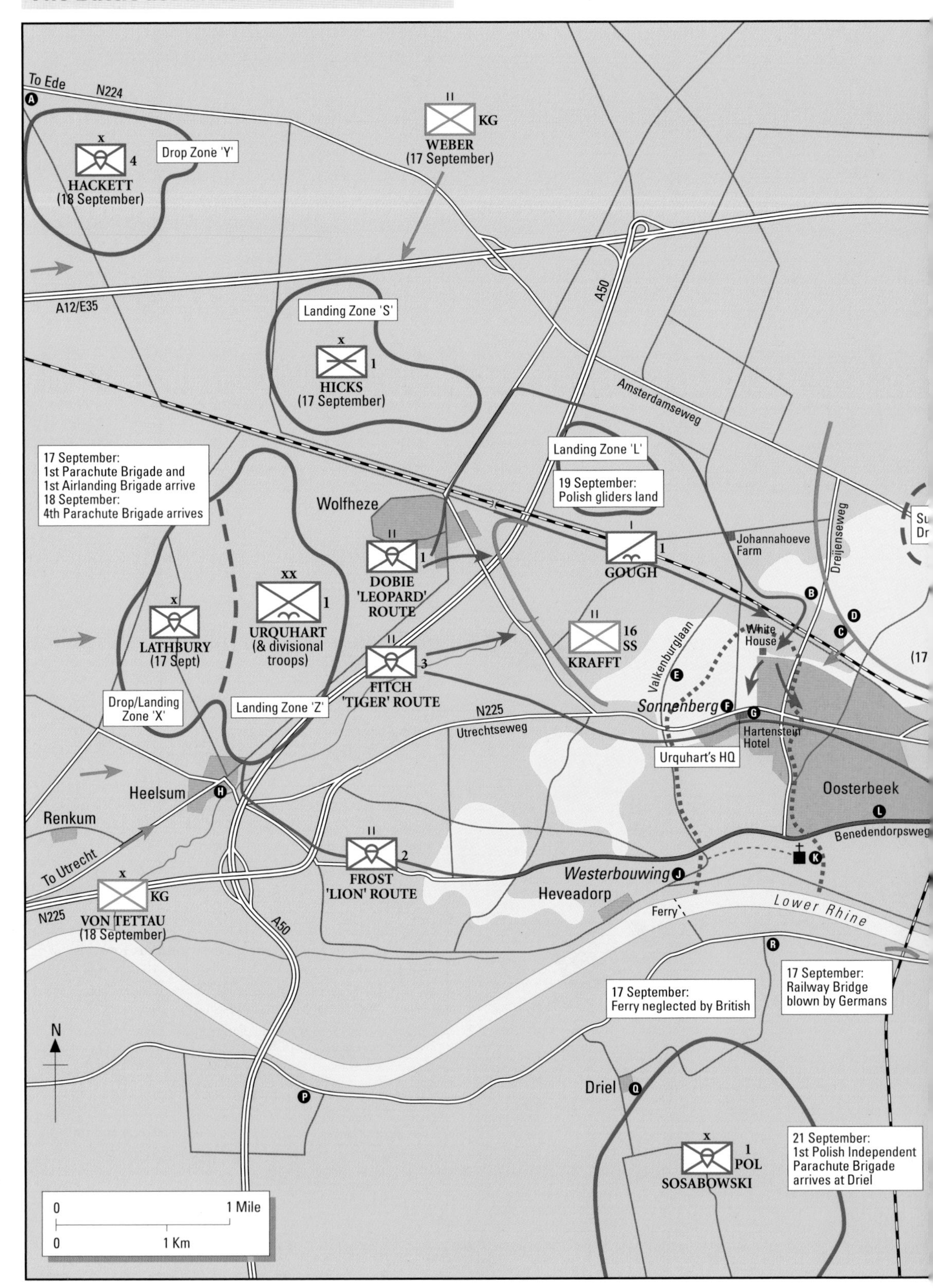

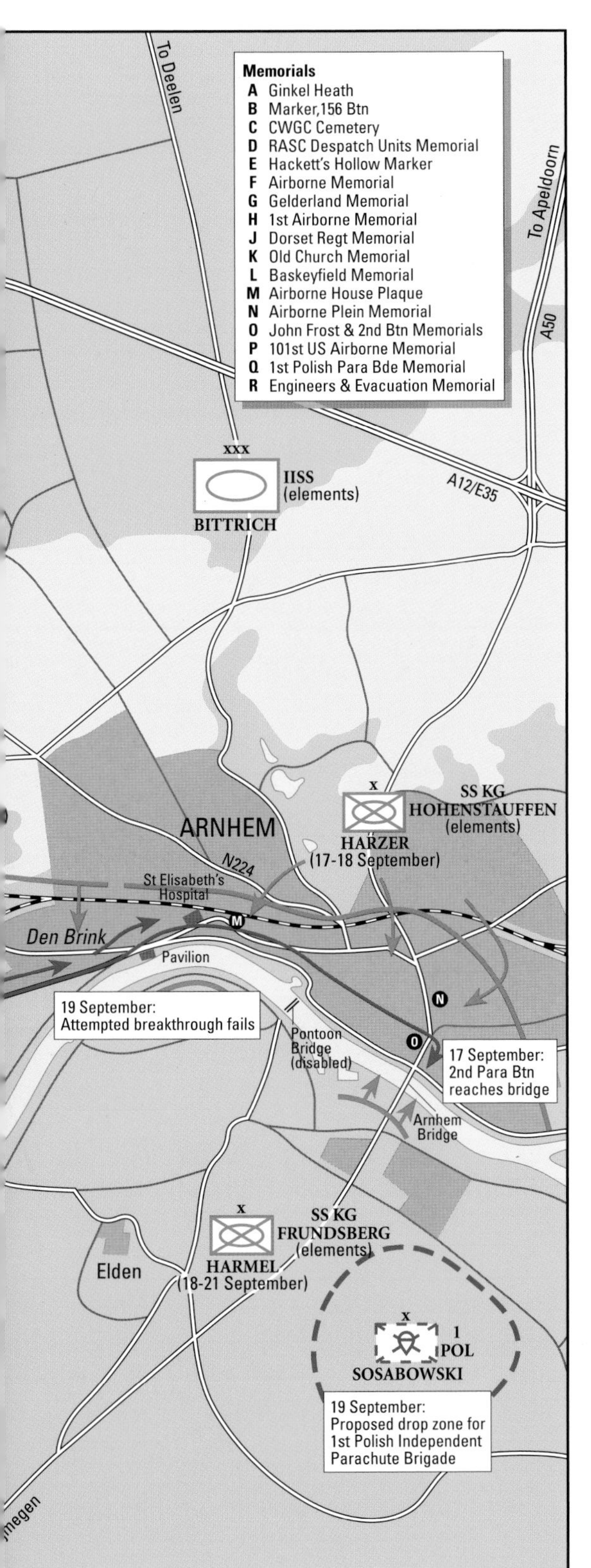

Museums

Airborne Museum Hartenstein
Utrechtseweg 232, 6862 AZ Oosterbeek
Telephone: [00 31] (0)26 333 7710
www.airbornemuseum.com
Housed in the 1st Airborne Divisional HQ, the museum records the Battle of Arnhem and of Oosterbeek. Plans, photographs, weapons and equipment are on display and a series of wonderfully accurate dioramas give a vivid picture of the events of September 1944. There are video screens showing original footage from British, German and Dutch sources and three-dimensional aerial photographs.
Open: Sundays and public holidays, 12 noon to 5 p.m. Monday to Saturday April to October 10 a.m. to 5 p.m; November to March 11 a.m. to 5 p.m. Closed 25 December and 1 January.

Liberation Museum (Bevrijdingsmuseum)
Wylerbaan 4, 6560 AC Groesbeek
Telephone: [00 31] (0)24 397 4404
The story of the Liberation is told in three sections: the inter-war period 1918–40, the Occupation 1940–44 and the Liberation 17 September 1944 – 5 May 1945, with excellent coverage of Market Garden. In the Dome of Honour the names of the Allied service men and women who died in north-western Europe between 6 June 1944 (D-Day) and 8 May 1945 (VE-Day) are recorded.
Open: Sundays and public holidays, 12 noon to 5 p.m. Monday to Saturday 10 a.m. to 5 p.m. Closed 25 December and 1 January.

National War and Resistance Museum (Nationaal Oorlogs- en Verzetsmuseum)
Museumpark 1, 5825 AM Overloon
Telephone: [00 31] (0)478 641250 (including guided tour bookings)
www.oorlogsmuseum.nl
'War belongs in a museum' is the motto here. Life in an occupied country is portrayed and the realities of oppression, collaboration and resistance are shown, both in Europe and the Far East. The park has military aircraft, tanks and other heavy equipment.
Open: Daily, July to August 10 a.m. to 6 p.m., September to June 10 a.m. to 5 p.m. Closed 24, 25 and 31 December and 1 January.

Viewpoints: The countryside in which the Battle of Arnhem took place can be appreciated from the Eusebius Tower, Kerkplein 1, Arnhem (open Tuesday to Saturday 10 a.m. to 5 p.m. and Sunday 12 noon to 5 p.m). The Oosterbeek enclave should be viewed from the Westerbouwing restaurant as well as toured using the information on the plan opposite. The sites of other aspects of Operation Market Garden are marked on the map on the back cover. A good road map and street plans of the towns (from VVV – tourist information – offices) will also be needed.

Cemeteries: Most of the fallen of the 1st Airborne and supporting units, as well as those of XXX Corps killed south of the Rhine, are buried in Oosterbeek, as are those who fell during the final liberation of the area in April 1945. Those with no known graves are recorded at the CWGC Canadian Cemetery near Groesbeek. American dead not repatriated are buried at Margraten, just east of Maastricht.

Left: Major-General R.E. Urquhart (right) and his Chief-of-Staff Lt-Colonel C.B. Mackenzie confer on the terrace of the Hartenstein Hotel, Oosterbeek. (IWM)

Right: Walking wounded being evacuated on 20 September from the medical dressing station which had been set up in the Hotel Vreewijk. The AFV is a German self-propelled gun. (B)

20 September – 1st British Airborne

At the bridge in Arnhem the night passed with few incidents, giving way to a grey, drizzling dawn. The Germans now had freedom of movement in the town and artillery fire came in from all sides. The Germans also tried to get under the northern ramp of the bridge from the east to fix explosives, and a series of sharp actions took place during which Lt Jack Grayburn was killed. He was awarded the VC posthumously. The anti-tank guns could no longer be manned and tanks dominated the roadways. Frost was wounded and had to hand over the command to Gough. By the end of the afternoon the Germans could move freely over the bridge. As darkness fell the Brigade HQ building was on fire and a truce was arranged to evacuate the many wounded. The houses burned in the night; just a few men held on, with no hope of relief.

The western side of the Oosterbeek salient was held by the 1st Border, from Westerbouwing north up to the Sonnenberg on the Utrechtseweg. North of them various small units held the Valkenburglaan, past the modern sports centre, the line turning east along the road to the White House (the Dreyeroord Hotel) near the railway station and held, from 11 p.m., by the KOSB. But Hackett, with the remnants of 4th Brigade, was outside the line to the north west. They made for Oosterbeek and 60 men of the 10th Battalion broke through at about 1.30 p.m. The 156th were pinned down in a hollow now marked by a memorial on the road opposite the riding stables. Of the 150 men who started the bayonet charge, between 50 and 60 reached the perimeter in Oosterbeek.

The main German effort was by 9th SS Panzer, in the east along the riverside. Lt-Colonel Thompson, commanding the Light Regiment, had his 75-mm guns near the old church on Benedendorpsweg and had rallied retreating men of the South Staffords and the 1st, 3rd and 11th Battalions the previous evening to hold the sector. A group under Major Lonsdale was positioned halfway between the church and the railway bridge. On Wednesday Lonsdale Force came under heavy attack. L-Sgt John Baskeyfield continued to fight his 6-pounder anti-tank gun against tanks and SPGs after all his team had been killed, until he too lost his life. He was awarded the VC. Eventually the remains of the force had to be withdrawn to positions close to the church, where Lonsdale paid tribute to them.

In the centre of the eastern flank, along the Utrechtseweg, there was a gap in the line where two hotels, the Schoonoord and the Vreewijk, were in use as medical dressing stations (MDS). An approach by German tanks had been stopped dead and fortunately no further attempt was made there that day. The developing salient was further isolated when the cables of the ferry were cut to prevent use by the Germans. That day's supply drop delivered only 13% of its load into British hands.

20 September – 82nd and 101st US Airborne and XXX Corps

To the south twin problems beset the relieving force. German attacks at Son and Veghel threatened the precious road, but Taylor's men and XXX Corps encircled their enemies and cleared the highway. At Nijmegen the battle for the bridges was renewed with 504th Regiment and the Irish Guards making for the railway bridge on the west and 505th with the Grenadier Guards headed for the road bridge on the east while Gavin was also repulsing a German attack from the east at Beek. By noon 504th were at the riverside, but the boats they needed were still coming up from the rear. By 3 p.m. the Grenadiers had taken the fortress of Valkhof and to their left 504th were ready to embark.

The crossing of the Waal was a remarkable feat of arms. Not only is the river wide, but beyond it the Americans had to cross an equally broad flood plain bounded by the heavily defended dike. Their casualties afloat were severe and once ashore the furious paratroopers swept the Germans ruthlessly aside, poured through the strongpoint based on an ancient redoubt and put the defenders of the northern ends of the bridges to flight. By 7 p.m. the first tanks were clanking over the road bridge and into Lent, but there they halted to refuel and rearm, and, to the fury of the Americans, there they stayed all night.

Below: The memorial to the crossing of the Waal by the 504th Regiment, 82nd US Airborne, stands on the dike on the north bank at the place where their courageous exploit was carried out. (MME)

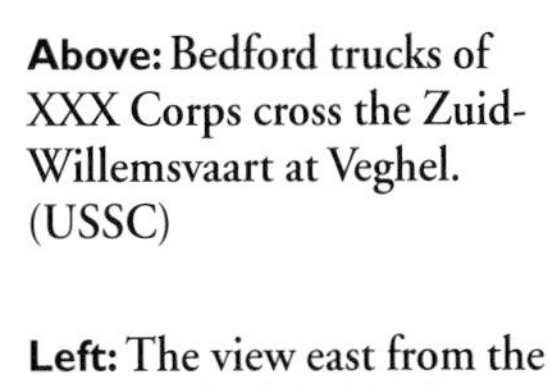

Above: Bedford trucks of XXX Corps cross the Zuid-Willemsvaart at Veghel. (USSC)

Left: The view east from the dike north of the Waal at Nijmegen. The railway bridge is at the right and the trees at the left conceal the 18th-century redoubt. The exposure of the 504th to enemy fire was extreme, but they crossed the river and smashed the German defence. (MME)

Below: Stirlings of No. 38 Group RAF dropping supply containers at Doorwerth. RASC Air Despatch were responsible for handling the supplies and a memorial to those who lost their lives stands north of the Arnhem Oosterbeek War Cemetery. (AM)

21 September – 1st British Airborne

With the last resistance at Arnhem road bridge ceasing at about 5 a.m. the Germans could concentrate their attention on the reduction of Oosterbeek. Model gave overall command to Bittrich who put Harzer of 9th SS Panzer in charge. Reinforcements, including 506th Heavy Tank Battalion with 60 tanks, were arriving. The battle of the Cauldron began.

The troops on the west under Von Tettau were of very variable quality, but included a battalion of the Luftwaffe's Hermann Goering NCO School with some pre-war tanks. These were the men that B Company, 1st Border faced that morning and the three platoons could not hold their ground on the eminence of Westerbouwing. The Germans paid a high price for their success, losing their tanks to PIAT fire and unable to push further forward than the gasworks. They left the remnants of B Company, now part of an ad hoc formation called Breeseforce under Major Breese, solidly in control of the south-eastern flank, but overlooked from the height of Westerbouwing from which shell and mortar fire could be directed on the British.

On the opposite side of the salient vigorous German attacks made no progress but inflicted more losses. Lonsdale Force became the operational unit for this sector with the

Right: The position of the 3-inch mortar of the 1st Battalion, Border Regiment south of Lennepweg was overlooked by the Germans on the height to the west. On the left Private R. Tierney, on the right Sergeant McDowell and out of frame left Private N. Knight. (IWM)

Below: German troops fire on descending paratroops. (From a German film, IWM)

Left: A Bren-gunner of the 1st Polish Independent Parachute Brigade takes up a defensive position at Driel. The Germans failed to dislodge the Poles, but there was little the Poles could do to aid their comrades north of the river. (PISM)

men of the Glider Pilot Regiment, unlike the Americans a full-fledged fighting force, adding to their modest strength. Here Major Cain of the South Staffords earned his VC. To their north on the Utrechtseweg, beyond a gap mercifully not attacked, 10th Battalion had been deployed east of the MDS as a blocking line and it was on them that the strength of the 9th SS Panzer fell. The front line crept towards the crossroads. In the north, late in the afternoon, it was the KOSB's turn. A determined assault drove them half out of the White House precincts, but a yet more determined counter-attack took back the lost ground. The cost, however, had been heavy and when night fell they withdrew to fresh positions further west.

The Oosterbeek perimeter had now taken a shape that would endure to the last. Groups of Glider Pilots, Recce Squadron, Pathfinders and other divisional troops fought alongside the thinning ranks of the three brigades sent to take the bridge at Arnhem. But hope there was. Contact had at last been made with the artillery of XXX Corps and shellfire of remarkable accuracy now supported the defenders. Moreover, at 5.15 p.m. the 1st Polish Independent Parachute Brigade landed near Driel, south of the river. They had been held up by bad weather for days and landed under fire with only two-thirds of their number. The ferry had gone by now, and when they approached the river heavy fire from the lost height of Westerbouwing drove them back. There was little they could do but dig in and await German retaliation.

21 September - 82nd and 101st US Airborne and XXX Corps

The land between the Waal and the Lower Rhine is low, wet and webbed with roads raised on dikes. When the Irish Guards at last moved forward they were easy targets for the guns of 10th SS Panzer at Elst. Infantry attempts to outflank the defence failed and the advance stalled. Radio contact with the Typhoons which had cleared the road further south was never established and air support was thus lacking. Night fell with no gain.

Above: From the old church, the view to the east. In September 1944 this place was the centre of the resistance of Lonsdale Force. (MME)

Left: From Westerbouwing the dominance of the German position here can be appreciated. The railway bridge is to the right and, in the distance, the white top of the road bridge arch is visible. (MME)

22 September - 1st British Airborne

The arrival of the Polish paratroops relieved the immediate pressure on the Oosterbeek perimeter. German units that might otherwise have attacked were sent south of the river to prevent a possible Polish assault on the southern end of the bridge and on the road to Nijmegen. But German ammunition was plentiful and a constant rain of mortar fire and shelling steadily depleted the manpower at Urquhart's disposal. Snipers and probing infantry attacks contributed to their losses.

The houses of the civilians became thronged with refugees and the wounded of both sides. Just west of the old church Kate ter Horst's house was so packed with casualties that the newly wounded were laid outside next to the dead. The devotion and courage of the Dutch astounded the soldiers who had made their homes a wasteland.

The same terrain that hampered the Allied advance protected the Polish force at Driel. Lacking anti-tank guns, which had landed in gliders north of the Rhine, their PIATs inflicted severe damage on German tanks unable to manoeuvre away from the dike-top roads. Two of Urquhart's officers crossed the river to tell Sosabowski that an attempt to get some of his men across the river would be made that night using rubber boats. First contact with XXX Corps was also achieved when three scout cars of the Household Cavalry managed to pass round the western flank of the German positions by minor roads. They were followed by some tanks of the 4th/7th Royal Dragoons and Bren carriers of the 5th Duke of Cornwall's Light Infantry.

Today the river is a tamed beast; a lock and an artificial island stand below the Westerbouwing heights. In 1944 the water flowed swift and free, a real obstacle even to experienced boatmen. The plan to haul a gaggle of boats over on a cable failed, and attempts to row over with the tiny paddles achieved little success. Only 52 Poles got over before the operation was halted.

22 September - XXX Corps

The journey of XXX Corps to meet the Poles had been eventful. The Household Cavalry had moved west and north from the Nijmegen bridgehead in the morning mist, but behind them the 7th Somerset Light Infantry came under heavy fire as they approached the village of Oosterhout. It was not until heavy artillery and tank support was brought to bear that the village was taken. By then it was 4.30 p.m., but the road was open and the 4th/7th Dragoons took only 30 minutes to reach the Poles at Driel. Others followed, brushing off a party of German tanks making an attempt to attack westwards from Elst. But there were no boats and no way over to Oosterbeek.

Left: Men of the Household Cavalry reached the Poles at Driel in the afternoon of 22 September in three Daimler Dingo armoured cars. This put Major-General S.F. Sosabowski in radio contact with Lt-General Horrocks, but that was all. (IWM)

Left: Evidence of the fighting required to keep Hell's Highway open is clear in this photograph, taken on 28 September, of men of the 101st Airborne making their way through Uden. (USSC)

22 September - 101st US Airborne

Model had ordered Generaloberst Student to cut Hell's Highway at Veghel on the Willems Canal using the 59th Infantry Division from the west and Kampfgruppe Walther from the east. Taylor, unlike the British, made use of the intelligence provided by the Dutch Resistance and was forewarned. Veghel was lightly defended by a battalion of 501st Regiment and Uden entirely undefended. From Son, 506th Regiment moved through Veghel for Uden that morning and their advance party met the Germans coming in from the east. So convincing a show of strength was offered that the Germans turned south along the road to join the main attack on Veghel.

By chance Brigadier-General Anthony McAuliffe, the 101st's artillery commander, was in Veghel. With the same determination he was to show at Bastogne the following winter he deployed the newly arriving men of 506th and of 327th Glider Infantry. The attack from the north was halted and a thrust from the canal bridge driven off by 506th and the 44th Royal Tanks.

The German attack from the west ran into an American operation by 501st and 502nd Regiments and thus failed to mesh with their comrades from the east. Colonel Howard Johnson achieved the near impossible in converting attack to defence and held the road south of the canal. As Gavin's 82nd Airborne had the situation east of Nijmegen well under control, Horrocks ordered the Grenadier and Coldstream Guards to turn south once more to clear the road from Uden to Veghel, restore his vital lines of supply and lever open the jaws of what was becoming a trap.

Below: In the Oosterbeek enclave resupply was vital, but most of the tonnage so valiantly delivered fell into enemy hands. Signals about the precise location of the British had not reached England. Here, in the grounds of the Hartenstein Hotel, men of the 1st Airborne make frantic signals to approaching aircraft to show their true positions. (IWM)

Below: North of the Airborne Museum in the former Hartenstein Hotel stands the Airborne Memorial. Sculpted panels around the base depict the events of September 1944, including this, symbolising the succour rendered to the wounded by the women of Oosterbeek. (MME)

23 September – 1st British Airborne

The German's grip at Oosterbeek was relentless. Shelling, sniping and probing raids continued and the wounded sheltering in the houses and the MDSs at the Stationsweg crossroads grew in number. The last of the resupply flights achieved no more than its predecessors, eight of the aircraft were lost and the material dropped fell into German hands. Still the perimeter held.

Boats were to be brought up for a Polish crossing that night. They did not arrive until midnight and came without the skilled men to handle them. What is more, they held only 12 men each instead of the 16 expected, so the Poles had to reorganise in darkness and under fire. Only 153 made it into the perimeter.

Right: A Bren-gun crew of C Company, 1st Border, protect the western flank of the enclave on 23 September. They were subjected to continuous sniper fire and German attempts at infiltration. (IWM)

Below: Some supply drops made it. This container is coming down on the open space north of the Hartenstein on which the Airborne Memorial now stands. (IWM)

23 September – XXX Corps and 101st US Airborne

The position to the south appeared to be improving with Elst now under attack by the British and McAuliffe repelling a renewed attack on Veghel. He was then able to push two battalions of 506th Regiment north to meet the Guards and by 3 p.m. the road was open once more. Reinforcement and resupply by air was successful. But still the sense of urgency was lacking; while apparently unaware of just how critical the situation at Oosterbeek was, Horrocks, Browning and their staffs appeared deaf to all attempts to acquaint them with reality.

24 September – 1st British Airborne and XXX Corps

In the Oosterbeek pocket the plight of the wounded in the MDSs at the crossroads was becoming extreme. Colonel Warrack, the senior medical officer, got Urquhart's permission to seek a truce to allow them to be evacuated. Together with the Dutch liaison officer, Lt-Commander Wolters, he succeeded in meeting Bittrich who immediately agreed and some 450 men were moved into German care.

Some air support was now given to the hard-pressed defenders and casualties were somewhat reduced, but hope of relief was fast fading.

Horrocks viewed the situation with Sosabowski from the tower of Driel church and then the Polish commander found himself at a meeting with Horrocks and Lt-General Thomas of the 43rd Division. He was furious to be ordered to put his 1st Battalion under Thomas's orders to follow a crossing of the river beneath Westerbouwing by the 4th Dorset Regiment that night. He pointed out the extreme danger of such an enterprise, but was silenced. The alternative of evacuating 1st Airborne was under consideration at the same time. The assault boats were late and, when they arrived, too few. The Dorsets would cross alone, and three hours late, early on Monday morning.

Right: The memorial to the 4th Dorset Regiment's men who crossed the river in the early hours of 25 September. It is on the western end of the south-facing wall of the restaurant at Westerbouwing. Sosabowski had spoken strongly against the operation, proposing instead a crossing in greater numbers further downstream, where there was a real prospect of being unopposed. When he learned that the boats required were far in the rear his criticism was robust. Of the 315 Dorsets who crossed, 13 died and about 200 were taken prisoner. (MME)

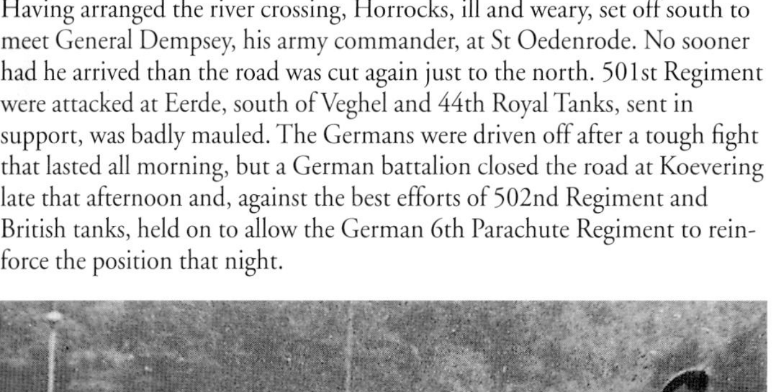

24 September – 101st US Airborne and XXX Corps

Having arranged the river crossing, Horrocks, ill and weary, set off south to meet General Dempsey, his army commander, at St Oedenrode. No sooner had he arrived than the road was cut again just to the north. 501st Regiment were attacked at Eerde, south of Veghel and 44th Royal Tanks, sent in support, was badly mauled. The Germans were driven off after a tough fight that lasted all morning, but a German battalion closed the road at Koevering late that afternoon and, against the best efforts of 502nd Regiment and British tanks, held on to allow the German 6th Parachute Regiment to reinforce the position that night.

Below: In the midst of modern housing and shops, the memorial to the 1st Independent Polish Parachute Brigade is part of the daily life of Driel. (MME)

Above: After the war Major-General Sosabowski at last rides the Driel ferry, in the company of the ferryman, Peter Hensen. The ferry was ignored during the advance on 17 September and the cables were cut on the 20th. (PISM)

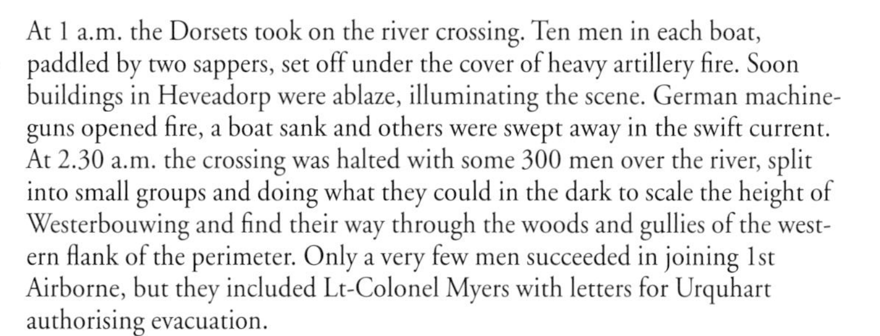

25 September – XXX Corps and 1st British Airborne

At 1 a.m. the Dorsets took on the river crossing. Ten men in each boat, paddled by two sappers, set off under the cover of heavy artillery fire. Soon buildings in Heveadorp were ablaze, illuminating the scene. German machine-guns opened fire, a boat sank and others were swept away in the swift current. At 2.30 a.m. the crossing was halted with some 300 men over the river, split into small groups and doing what they could in the dark to scale the height of Westerbouwing and find their way through the woods and gullies of the western flank of the perimeter. Only a very few men succeeded in joining 1st Airborne, but they included Lt-Colonel Myers with letters for Urquhart authorising evacuation.

25 September – 1st British Airborne

Ignorance of the failure of the Dorsets' gallant attack fed the belief that two evacuation crossing points would be available, one where the Dorsets had crossed and one, the route actually used, approached by a path west of the church. The evacuation was to start with the troops in the north of the perimeter, and the flanking forces at the river-side would be last.

During the day Lonsdale Force was again hard pressed by German attacks, but held them off, and the KOSB stopped another attempt in the north in its tracks. After dark the little groups made their silent way towards the river to queue patiently to board the boats. Sappers of 260th (Wessex) Field Company were there in paddled assault boats and men of 23rd Canadian Field Company in their powered storm boats. In the relentless rain the ferries plied back and forth, the foul weather and continuous pounding of British artillery concealing the operation from the Germans. As dawn approached some men attempted to swim across fully clothed and drowned. Downstream, the boats at the other crossing point found only the odd survivor to rescue and were too late to supplement the real evacuation. Still there were men waiting to get away, and at about 5.30 a.m. the last Canadian boat, under heavy German fire, got back with all occupants wounded. Some 300 men were left behind in addition to the wounded. Of 11,000 men who had landed north of the river fewer than 2,300 were evacuated.

25 September – 101st US Airborne and XXX Corps

In the grey rain the battle along the road continued. Fierce fighting was taking place at Koevering where 506th Regiment and 44th Royal Tanks were pressing from the north and British reinforcements from the south. By the end of the day the Germans had been forced to withdraw and the road was open again.

Left: 101st US Airborne south of the Rhine in October 1944. A memorial to them stands almost under the south-east end of the autoroute bridge. (USSC)

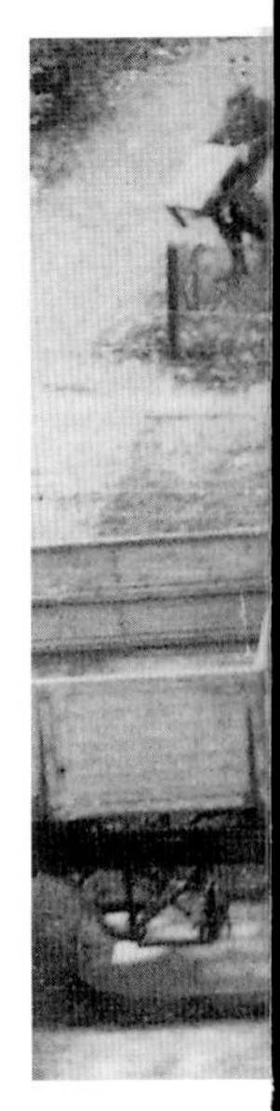

Right: The sack of Arnhem. A clandestine photograph of Germans looting the houses in Jacob Marislaan. (De Booys/AM)

Above: Captain Barry Ingram, 1st Border, was caught attempting to escape in civilian clothes in Weverstraat, Oosterbeek, on 26 September. Others succeeded. (AM)

Right: The evacuation route. On the right, beyond the river, is the old church. The water now flows quietly – in 1944 the untamed Rhine was a formidable obstacle. (MME)